First Facts®

DATA MANIA

Pigs, Cows, and Probability

I'm Matt Maticus. I love mathematics! Probability is an important part of math. Join me on the farm, and I'll show you how!

by Marcie Aboff

Consultant:
Michele Koomen, PhD
Co-Chair and Assistant Professor of Education
Gustavus Adolphus College
St. Peter, Minnesota

CAPSTONE PRESS
a capstone imprint

First Facts is published by Capstone Press,
151 Good Counsel Drive, P.O. Box 669, Mankato, Minnesota 56002.
www.capstonepub.com

032010
005742LKF10

 Books published by Capstone Press are manufactured with paper
containing at least 10 percent post-consumer waste.

Library of Congress Cataloging-in-Publication Data
Aboff, Marcie.
  Pigs, cows, and probability / by Marcie Aboff.
     p. cm.—(First facts. Data mania)
  Summary: "Uses animals on a farm to explore how using probability can help readers
form conclusions about the likelihood of future events"—Provided by publisher.
  Includes bibliographical references and index.
  ISBN 978-1-4296-4529-4 (library binding)
  1. Probabilities—Juvenile literature. I. Title. II. Series.

  QA273.16.A26 2011
  519.2—dc22   2010000551

Editorial Credits
Christopher L. Harbo, editor; Matt Bruning, designer and illustrator; Eric Manske,
    production specialist

Photo Credits
iStockphoto: Alex Varlakov, 19 (cow), Carlos Andres, cover (blackboard), Stilyan Savov,
    background (throughout)
Shutterstock: Alistar Scott, 15 (dog), Dmitriy Shironosov, 11 (white hen), Eric Isselée, 11
    (brown hen), 14, Givaga, 11 (white eggs), Iakov Kalinin, 11 (grass), 13 (sunrise),
    imantsu, 7 (horse), Inc, 7, 9 (green apple), J. Helgason, 17 (box), James Steidl, 13
    (rooster), Jiri Pavlik, 15 (orange toy bottom), Matthew Jacques, 5 (farm), Mushakesa,
    21 (thought balloon), Nata Sdobnikova, 15 (toys top), Nattika, 11 (brown eggs),
    NicolasMcComber, 21 (rawhide toy), Nitr, 7, 9 (red apple), Olga Bogatyrenko, cover
    (cow), Pichugin Dmitry, 9 (horse), Serg64, 11 (sky), Sergej Razvodovskij, 19 (milk
    bucket), skeletoriad, 15 (blue toy bottom), Valery Shklovskiy, 21 (dog), vhrinchenko,
    11 (fence), Viktor Gmyria, 13 (clock), Viorel Sima, 17 (cow)

Table of Contents

What Are the Chances?

It's feeding time and the cows are hungry. Farmer Bob just gave them fresh grain. Is it more likely or less likely the cows are eating right now? If you said more likely, you're right. You used **probability** to figure out if something is happening.

probability—the likelihood of something happening or being true

The Power of Prediction

Crunch, crunch! The farm's horse loves munching apples. Can you **predict** which color of apple the horse will eat next? Let's **compare** the apples. The horse has six red apples and two green apples. Is it more or less likely she will pick a green apple? The answer is less likely because there are fewer green apples.

predict—to say what you think will happen in the future
compare—to judge one thing against another

Pie Graphs

A pie graph is a circular chart that is broken into sections. This pie graph uses red pieces to show the red apples. Green pieces show the green apples. The pie graph helps you compare information about the whole group of apples.

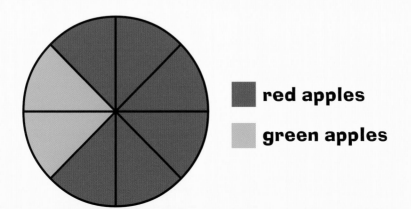

■ red apples

■ green apples

Now the horse has four green apples and four red apples. Is it more or less likely the horse will pick a green apple? The amount of red apples and green apples is the same. The horse has an **equal** chance of picking either a red apple or a green apple.

equal—the same as something else in size, value, or amount

four green apples

four red apples

9

Stick to the Facts

I love probability, and that's a fact! You can use facts to make predictions. For example, hens with white feathers and white **earlobes** lay only white eggs. Hens with dark feathers and dark earlobes lay only brown eggs. What is the chance a chicken with white earlobes will lay brown eggs?

earlobe—the soft, fleshy lower part of the outer ear

Past information also helps you determine the chance of something happening. Last week, the rooster crowed every day between 5:00 and 5:30 in the morning. Will he crow between the same times tomorrow morning? Based on the information, it is probable. Is there a chance he might crow before or after those times? Yes. It is possible but not probable.

probable—likely to happen or be true

13

Common Sense

Using common sense can also help you make predictions. Mama pig and her piglets are cooling off in the mud. What is the chance that Papa pig will fly over to join them? The answer is none because it's impossible. Pigs can't fly! But will Papa pig take a dip in the mud? Yes, I'm **certain** about that!

certain—sure that something will happen

Sorting

Sorting helps me predict what toys Max will play with today. I sorted his toys into two groups. The first group shows what toys Max plays with the most. The second group shows what toys he plays with the least. I predict Max will play with a toy from his favorite group. What do you think?

Max's favorite toys

Max's least favorite toys

Educated Guesses

Sometimes you must estimate to figure out the chance of something happening. When you estimate, you make a good guess.

The cows eat grain from a trough. Look at the size of the cows. Can you estimate how many cows can eat side-by-side at the trough?

estimate—to make a guess based on experience

How Many Cows Will Fit?

If you guessed four or five cows, you're probably right.

Farmer Bob estimates when he milks his cows. When he milks his first cow, he fills two buckets. Now he needs to milk three more cows. How many more buckets will he need? Based on the first cow, each cow can fill two buckets. Farmer Bob estimates that he will need six buckets for three more cows.

How Many Buckets?

  One cow fills
two buckets.

  Three cows should
fill six buckets.

19

Predict the Future

At the end of each day, Farmer Bob gives Max a bone. Will Max get a bone from Farmer Bob today? If you said yes, you're right! You've used past information to predict something will happen.

I know I've learned a lot about probability today. I predict you did too!

21

Glossary

certain (SUR-tuhn)—sure that something will happen

compare (kuhm-PAYR)—to judge one thing against another

earlobe (IHR-lohb)—the soft, fleshy lower part of the outer ear

equal (EE-kwuhl)—the same as something else in size, value, or amount

estimate (ESS-ti-mate)—to make a guess based on experience

predict (pri-DIKT)—to say what you think will happen in the future

probability (prob-uh-BIL-i-tee)—the likelihood of something happening or being true

probable (PROB-uh-buhl)—likely to happen or be true

Read More

Aboff, Marcie. *Analyzing Doggie Data.* Data Mania. Mankato, Minn.: Capstone Press, 2011.

Cohen, Marina. *Probability.* My Path to Math. New York: Crabtree Pub., 2010.

Leedy, Loreen. *It's Probably Penny.* New York: H. Holt, 2007.

Internet Sites

FactHound offers a safe, fun way to find Internet sites related to this book. All of the sites on FactHound have been researched by our staff.

Here's all you do:

Visit *www.facthound.com*

FactHound will fetch the best sites for you!

Index